THE DOS AND DON'TS OF
WORK TEAM COACHING

A comprehensive study of the
worker/coach interpersonal relationship

Steve Herbelin, editor

Pat Guiney, associate editor

Original cartoons by Randy Glasbergen

HERBELIN PUBLISHING • RIVERBANK, CALIFORNIA

THE DOS AND DON'TS OF WORK TEAM COACHING

Contributing writers: Donna Bush, Susan Campbell, Michelle Churchman, Tag Goulet, Pat Guiney, Steve Herbelin, Kelly McClymer, Jennie L. Phipps, Jen Ryan.

Cartoons: by Randy Glasbergen. Copyright © 1998, Herbelin Publishing. All rights reserved.

Management consultants: Charles Blanton, Fred Wieland.

Cover design and cartoon colorization by Image Services, Modesto, CA.

Published in Riverbank, California by Herbelin Publishing, P.O. Box 74, Riverbank, CA 95367. E-mail: herbelin@netfeed.com

Publisher's Cataloging in Publication
(Provided by Quality Books, Inc.)

The dos and don'ts of work team coaching: a comprehensive study of the worker/coach interpersonal relationship / Steve Herbelin, editor ; Pat Guiney, associate editor ; Randy Glasbergen, illustrator. -- 1st ed.
    p. cm.
    Preassigned LCCN: 97-77525
    ISBN: 0-9661319-4-0

1. Work groups. 2. Self-directed work groups. 3. Organizational effectiveness. I. Herbelin, Steve.

HD66.D67 1998   658.4'02
                  QBI98-223

Printed in the United States of America

Table of Contents

Part II: Building Teamwork

Epilogue

Part III: Mini Stories

Introduction

The Dos and Don'ts of Work Team Coaching examines work team coaching from perhaps the most important and most often overlooked perspective—the point of view of the workers themselves. It is designed to help you, as coach, develop better interpersonal relationships with your work team. This book will complement the tools and knowledge you already possess and reinforce the managerial mechanics of work team coaching. Our goal is to make your role as work team coach easier and to enhance your ability to lead effectively.

Workers are in a unique and vital position to see supervisory weaknesses and problems that their coaches, supervisors, and managers are sometimes unaware of, and they can offer valuable assessments of how to correct them. Unfortunately, except for lunch-break gossip among themselves, workers are usually reluctant to express criticism of management. Too often, they fear that their remarks will not be well received. This book seeks to open communication between workers and coaches by pointing out some areas in which workers tend to notice shortcomings in coaches and managers. Some of these problems are quite serious and some are less so; all should be addressed in order to optimize the worker/coach relationship.

The principles addressed in this book do not represent the views of organized labor or disgruntled employees. We set forth no revolutionary ideas, nor do we presume to represent all workers. We simply present a general perspective on the dos and don'ts of the worker/coach relationship, illustrated with real stories from our own workplace experiences, interviews with other workers, and anecdotes submitted to Herbelin Publishing. We believe that "every story paints a picture." Hopefully, each of these stories will illustrate its underlying principle more vividly than any textbook prose ever could.

We present some anecdotes that portray poor coaching techniques. Our intent is not to characterize coaches or supervisors as monsters, but to show that poor coaching can have monstrous consequences and can be avoided. Although some of our examples depict rather extreme situations, the fundamentals illustrated should be applied to common, everyday incidents. You will see that when it comes to work team coaching, little things matter.

Some material in this book is elementary, yet all of it addresses areas that at least some supervisors sometimes have problems with. Please don't take anything in this book too lightly, and don't take it too personally either. We omit many fundamental principles of work team coaching, as these are more or less universally understood and do not bear repeating. We also omit topics that do not bear directly on the worker/coach interpersonal relationship, and thus do not fall within the scope or purpose of this book.

The Coach

A company can never fulfill its earning potential without efficient productivity from its workers, yet management too often takes workers for granted. The role of the coach is to redress this problem by serving as a liaison between the institutional element of management and the human element of production in a business entity. Whereas management typically thinks in terms of x number of bodies to produce y units of product, coaches view workers as individual people with different abilities and needs. Coaches must simultaneously help carry out the goals of management in highly competitive markets and interact on an individual, personal level with the workers who will physically achieve those goals. The coach's role can be either the strongest or the weakest link in any organization.

Successful coaches are fully in harmony with management's priorities and directions, and they know what is expected of them and their work teams. Managerial barometers such as units per labor hour and costs per unit however, should not be the coach's driving concern. Coaches who become too preoccupied with statistics and charts can alienate workers rather than help them be productive. Production goals, efficiency and work quality are the important things. As long as your team is accountable and operating effectively, the other numbers should fall into place.

Since many workers have a natural aversion toward management, they often view coaches and supervisors with distrust and skepticism.[1] In response to this antagonistic relationship, managers tend to perceive a need for continuing supervisory control of workers.

Coaching is not about controlling workers, nor is it about allowing them complete freedom. Coaching is, foremost, the process of developing and nurturing trust. Coaches must take the first step in this process by believing in and trusting their workers. For example, coaches can demonstrate trust by openly sharing managerial information with their work teams. This practice is justified by the principle that a better-informed team is a better-performing team—a team that is privy to the company's goals and methodology will more intelligently adopt reasonable and meaningful goals of its own.

---

[1] "Employees say they trust their co-workers more than their bosses and feel companies don't listen to them."—Marlin Company Study, September 1, 1997. "This may be because of recent downsizing, restructuring or feelings of inequity."—Sigal Barsade, assistant professor at the Yale School of Management and co-author of the Marlin study.

This book sheds additional light on this problem. We must undertake a healing process to increase trust and cooperation between employees and their bosses.—ed.

Coaches must also submit their teams' concerns to management. They must be effective salespersons, able to persuade their superiors that the ideas, needs, and abilities of their work teams should weigh at least as heavily as accounting experiments, information systems, and other factors in the company's decision-making process.

As much as coaches are an arm of management reaching into the work teams, they are the means by which work teams can reach up into management. Coaches embrace management and workers alike and bring them together equally, as one.

By taking the opportunity to better the lives of those working with you, you will be rewarded with a less stressful, more enjoyable workday. Aim your energies in directions where you can effect change, and you will inspire those around you to do the same. We, the workers, will readily support you if we see that your goals and ours are the same.

You will advance further in your organization not by catering to those above you, but by serving those beneath you. If you allow your team a generous degree of autonomy, it will become increasingly self-sufficient. A void will then develop in your workday due to the reduction in supervisory duties. Rather than withdraw from the team, you should take this opportunity to increase your involvement on a higher level. Personal interaction, though perhaps less frequent, will nevertheless become more meaningful as you no longer are required to micromanage work projects. You will likely have extra time on your hands. Like nature, a well-run business abhors a vacuum; your superiors will no doubt begin delegating new responsibilities to you (if not more of *their* everyday responsibilities), thus providing you with the opportunity to develop new skills and to eventually advance within the company.

You must always be careful, however, to stay focused on the present tasks and challenges. Your work group is your workers will tend to seek higher levels of autonomy than others will. A team of unskilled workers that is subject to frequent personnel turnover or layoffs will likely agree to a relatively low level of autonomy. Technicians with highly specialized skills, however, will function better as a team and feel more comfortable with a high degree of empowerment, possibly even including an active role in the hiring process.

Human Resources managers would like to fill every position in a company with self-motivated workers with leadership abilities. They are always looking for thinkers and doers, people who can supervise themselves and work well with others. Realistically, however, we are living in a less-than-perfect world with less-than-perfect workers. We have less-than-perfect coaches, managers, and even less-than-perfect presidents. Nevertheless, if we try simply to take the steps necessary to *improve*, we will move in the direction of perfection.

As a coach, your job should be to enable your team members to move toward their potential, both as individuals and as a group. By teaching team members to trust and cooperate with each other, you can build a team that continuously evolves toward perfection. It is not enough to preach about teamwork or stand on the sidelines and act as a cheerleader. You must work with nuts and bolts to achieve whatever grand vision lies over the horizon for your work team. You'll have to join your own team, become a team player, and like every other member, place the team's goals above your own.

Ironically, the only way to develop a team beyond the sum of its individual parts is to nurture the individuality of each part. The best way to do this is by allowing each team member an identifiable role. Naturally, the team should choose its own leader to manage the internal affairs and functional operations of the team. Assistant team leader, secretary, safety representative and other positions that involve specific contributions to the team should also be chosen. Ideally, each position should be rotated periodically. Every team member should at the very least have a role, if not a specific title. One person may contribute to team meetings by encouraging others to present their own ideas. Another may be adept at training new workers or obtaining supplies. All team members should, at one time or another, be part of special task teams. The coach should always be on the alert for team members' aptitudes and potentials. With the proper encouragement, everyone will eventually function in a specific role within the group and take on varying capacities of leadership. When individual team members know that they fulfill a vital role, their cumulative efforts engender a team spirit that results in greater efficiency and ultimately, increased profits for the company.

Work team empowerment is the challenge of the present and the wave of the future in business. Coaches and managers who are involved in this difficult yet vitally important process should always keep in mind Reinhold Niebuhr's *Serenity Prayer (1943)*. Although you may have read this before, please don't skip over it. Read it again, and remember it always: *"God, give us the grace to accept with serenity the things that cannot be changed, courage to change the things which should be changed, and the wisdom to distinguish the one from the other."*

We hope you find the following *Dos and Don'ts* informative, interesting, and thought-provoking.

–Herbelin Publishing

vehicle. To stay on course, you must keep your eyes on the road ahead. You must know where you and your team (or teams) are going, and how to get there. Your desire to advance in the company's hierarchy must be held in check while you focus on your present responsibilities. Sports fans know what often happens when a team looks ahead to the "big game" down the road—a lesser opponent wipes them out along the way. The same fate can befall a coach who is not fully attuned to his or her immediate challenge.

> "I won't be a line coach for long," Joshua boasted. "I'll be in management before you know it, making the really *big* bucks." He was right on two of his three predictions: Joshua is now an assistant manager at a car wash somewhere.
> —*anonymous auto factory worker*

Three Coaching Qualities

There are countless different coaching styles. A coach may be task-oriented or people-oriented. He or she may be autocratic, diplomatic, democratic, intuitive, by-the-book, or off-the-cuff. Proactive or passive. Permissive or strict. Ideally, a coach should be able to "surf" from one style to another according to the nature of the particular job and shifting circumstances. Whatever the style, a coach must possess and continually develop the following three personal qualities, each of which is equally important and complements the others:

Competence: In order to maintain the trust and cooperation of his workers, a coach must possess suitable expertise in his field. Technical know-how, however, does not automatically translate into competence. Competence also includes factors such as dealing with customers, managing time effectively and following through on commitments. A deficiency in technical knowledge can be overcome by skills in management and superior coaching abilities.

Personality: Competence will give you the authority to lead others, but only for a limited time. Without the right personality, you will eventually lose the attention and respect of your workers. An engaging, friendly personality will lead people to trust you, believe in you, and follow you. If they like you, they will cooperate with you.

Empathy: Your workers will grow wary of you if they sense there is no substance behind your pleasant, charming personality. You must empathize with your workers. Let them know that you are "all in the same boat," that the outcome of a project has the same level of importance for everyone involved. Always maintain the highest ethical standards in your treatment of others. You must be, and be perceived as, honest and assertive. In order to maintain your ability to influence and persuade others, you must be known for your unwavering trustworthiness and fairness. Rather than follow the philosophy that "the end justifies the means," consider the effect that the means have in terms of the interests and well-being of your workers.

Teamwork and Empowerment

Teamwork is nothing new. Could you imagine making an animated cartoon without teamwork? How about a skyscraper? You can't even mow your lawn by yourself, because it took a team to bring the mower into existence. About the only thing you can do by yourself is . . . well, I won't mention it.

—agricultural field worker Adan Aguinigas

Workers who function together in self-directed, empowered work teams play a more active role in the decision-making process and therefore have a more personal stake in the company's performance. Empowerment gives workers a sense of individual freedom and control over their destinies that translates into increased job satisfaction, higher employee morale, and hopefully, increased company performance. In recent years, progressive organizations have been trying to set up the use of empowered work teams. Some, like General Motors and Procter and Gamble, have made significant progress in this effort and have reaped substantial profit from it. For many others, the team concept remains largely just that—simply a *concept*, an idea. Adapting to change requires effort and patience on the part of both workers and management. Workers, coming from a long tradition of being told what to do and how to do it, cannot learn how to manage their own tasks overnight. Competent coaching must provide the guidance. Top management must provide the commitment.

In order to successfully implement empowered work teams, managers must have the courage and stamina to allow teams to become self-directing. Often, middle managers are hesitant to abandon the control that they have traditionally wielded over employees. When they see work teams becoming autonomous, they sometimes reassert their own power by ignoring or sabotaging the empowerment process. This problem faces many businesses as they attempt to make the transition to self-directed work groups, and is exemplified by the following story submitted to Herbelin Publishing:

Continuous Quality Improvement became all the rage in our hospital administration last year. The principle of this managing technique is to involve the workers in the decision-making process, thereby giving them "ownership" and responsibility for a procedure or process.

Our hospital spent lots of money sending its 360 employees to ten training sessions. The technique sounds great, but has one major flaw: it can't be used if middle management still insists on controlling.

A problem in the laboratory needed a solution. The doctors wanted their patients' results charted more promptly. In one of our quarterly lab meetings, we created a "Continuous Quality Improvement Team" to tackle the problem. We delegated five employees to the team, and then our supervisor appointed herself to the team as "facilitator."

At our first meeting we got together, brainstormed solutions, and came up with some possible plans. Our "facilitator" didn't seem too keen on any of them, but she didn't say so. Instead, she claimed we would have to have some way to measure the improvement between what we were currently doing to get reports on the chart, and what we would do if one of our plans was in place. We decided to study what we were doing now in a scientific manner before trying a new procedure.

That was the first and only Continuous Quality Improvement Team meeting. Another employee who was not on the team asked our supervisor several months later what had become of the team. She was told, "We're not going to meet anymore. All they wanted to do was make changes."

Modernizing the workforce, like any other retooling effort, requires a substantial investment of resources, both financial and otherwise. Allowances must be made for initial setbacks and inefficiencies while new processes and procedures are being learned. If a company is serious about teamwork and empowerment, it must stick to its decision without wavering back and forth. Companies that hesitate during the empowerment process risk causing worker indifference, which makes all future empowerment efforts much more difficult.

A work team can successfully achieve empowerment only if the workers are in some way involved with defining the terms of their own empowerment. Naturally, some kinds of

Part I

Building Trust

"I'm never wrong. I thought I was wrong
once . . . but I was wrong!"

(All stories and anecdotes used to illustrate *The Dos and Don'ts of Work Team Coaching* are real. However, some personal names and incidental facts have been fictionalized.)

Do: Be cordial

Going out of your way to say "Thanks" builds trust and cooperation. Don't hesitate to send a memo of thanks to another department.

> Our coach is the best coach in the world. Do you know why? Because he always says, "Thank you." I like that.

Likewise, say "Good morning" with a cheerful smile, even if you are preoccupied with work or if your feet hurt. Workers become embarrassed, hurt and angry when their cheerful greetings are not responded to in kind.

Always be courteous and show respect.

> I complained to my coach that he sometimes doesn't show enough respect for people. He told me, "You have to *earn* my respect." Later, I thought about that and realized that he has set up an unfortunate Catch-22 for himself.

Maybe only a few workers' performance is significantly affected by their coach's or supervisor's manners, but the combined effect of their output could harm—or enhance—overall company productivity.

Don't: Take yourself too seriously

Take the responsibilities of your job seriously, but don't take yourself too seriously. Don't let your supervisor's hat go to your head, so to speak.

> Dave used to be a really friendly guy and everyone liked him. Now he is our supervisor and he struts around like a proud rooster, expecting everyone to "hop to it" whenever he comes around. He has an attitude like, look at me, I'm a big shot. I avoid him because he doesn't care about me as a person anymore.

"Dave" may look in the mirror and say, "I have great hair, perfect posture, my father is a corporate CEO, and I'm all right in every way." Yet Dave may have accomplished nothing of lasting value in his lifetime, and contributed nothing to the betterment of society. His self-esteem is based on nothing but arrogance and egotism.

You might think that high self-esteem goes hand in hand with accomplishment and success, but that's not always the case. Often, individuals whose self-esteem is based on their inflated image of themselves react poorly when that self-image is challenged. In such cases, the person under attack is in conflict not only with his challenger but with himself as well. If a disgruntled worker were to approach Dave and say, "You know coach, you're a real jerk," Dave's fragile image of himself would be under threat. Dave might respond by striking out in anger, and doing whatever he could to restore his irrational perception of himself.

Psychiatrist Viktor Frankl, psychologist Barbara Lerner and others promote an alternative, healthier view of self-esteem. They suggest that an individual earn self-esteem by first achieving meaningful goals and accomplishing worthwhile things, then find self-realization by altogether forgetting the self in the service of others.

Coach "Donna" has climbed Mt. Everest, written six books on mountaineering, and participated in the Winter Olympics. She often speaks to youth groups about having confidence in themselves. Along the road to success, she has learned the vital lessons of humility and modesty.

When an employee approaches her and says, "You know Donna, you're a real jerk," she replies, "Okay, so what's your point?"

Test yourself. Imagine yourself in the above situation. Be honest—what would you do? Would you *react* to the situation, like Dave, or would you *interact* with the other person, like Donna?

Remember this: **Effective leaders always command respect; they never demand it.** Respect is a mutual thing—a person is not likely to have any more regard for you than you have for that person.

Do: Keep your ego in check

Being self-centered denies a person the ability to see most issues from a variety of perspectives. A successful leader must cast his ego aside in order to make fair and objective decisions.

> When I was a kid, I asked my Sunday school teacher, "What's ego?" His matter-of-fact answer was, "When you go to heaven, your ego is the part of you that gets left behind."
> As I've matured, those words have guided me successfully at work, at home and at play. They always keep me tuned in to who I am, and who I am not.

Foster an ability to laugh at yourself. It is a great human asset and a quality necessary for interactive personal relationships.

Remember this: **If you can't laugh at yourself, don't worry—others will do it for you.**

Don't: Be a know-it-all

While having a higher than average I.Q. is certainly an asset for a coach, having an excellent *social I.Q.* is even more important. Your job places you in a social environment where interpersonal skills take precedence over most any other kind of job skill.

> For the majority of our team, English is a second language, and none have a college degree. At a team meeting, our new coach gave this fancy speech full of big words about how to communicate effectively. After using the word "empathize" for about the third time, someone stopped him and said, "What does that word mean?" He looked around and asked if anyone knew what it meant.
>
> Sharon raised her hand and replied, "Yes. It means that if I were standing in your shoes, I wouldn't know what I was talking about!"

Most workers respect a good education yet resent brainy, know-it-all sorts. A manager or coach with scholarly mannerisms is a turnoff. Let us know that you are one of us. You have a family and a dog to support. You like to fish. Whatever it is. Remember, as coach, you've likely got as much or more to learn from us as we do from you. So, please don't talk down to us or try to dazzle us with your brilliance.

Some supervisors believe they must be perceived by their workers as knowing the answers to every question and being able to explain every situation. That's a bunch of hooey, though—with an attitude like that, your workers will sooner or later become skeptical of nearly everything you say. To build trust, be comfortable saying, "I don't know."

Do: Be "on the job" off the job

Maintain a high level of professionalism at all times, not only while working. Be aware of the possibility that someone you encounter off the job might someday walk into your office with a big account, or become CEO of your company. Even more importantly, acknowledge work acquaintances when you bump into them in public. You never know when an off-the-job encounter may come back to bless you (or haunt you) at work.

> We rarely see any of the big managers during graveyard shift. Every year on our last workday before Christmas, however, the "big wheels" come around and greet everyone. Like jolly elves, they wish everyone a merry Christmas and happy holidays. Last year, a few days after Christmas, I ran into the administrative manager at a supermarket. "Hello Brent," I said. He averted his eyes and failed to acknowledge my existence. I enjoy my work, but just don't feel comfortable at a place where the management has an attitude like they are on a plateau above everyone else. Ever since, I've been seeking another job.

Do: Be sociable

Keep up on things. Besides staying on top of what's going on with the company, keep abreast of the rest of the world by reading newspapers and magazines. Chat with your work team members about all kinds of things, not just work.

> I like it when my supervisor—I mean, *coach*—joins us for lunch. Even though she's never heard of the San Jose Lasers, she always has something interesting to talk about.

Everyone likes to feel important, and no one feels more important than when others show an interest in them. Ask "Mary" how her daughter's softball team is doing. Ask "John" about his fishing trip. Be careful not to overdo it, however. Workers are sensitive to instances when managers appear to pry into their lives, or worse yet, pretend to be interested when they really are not.

> My supervisor asked me the other day, "How's the family life?"
> "Fine," I said. He had asked me the same thing about a year earlier and I explained to him that I lost my wife and daughter in a car accident.

As you get to know your workers better, they will in turn feel more at ease with you and with their jobs.

Do: Maintain a positive sense of humor

Humor lightens everybody's load, making for a less stressful working day.

> On my birthday, the team surprised me with a beautifully decorated, layered cake at break time. When I handed a slice to Rick he said, "This reminds me of my job being your coach."
> "*Oh,*" I asked, "how is that?"
> He winked at me and said, "A piece of cake!"

Avoid dark or negative humor, especially personal attacks made in jest. Often, workers will respond to derisive ribbings with a weak smile, while inwardly resenting them. Excessive negative humor will result in your being perceived as "negative" in general, and will impair your ability to coach effectively.

> I like my coach, but I hate it when he calls me "short stuff." I told him so, and he still kept calling me that. When I asked him again to please stop, he said, "But Jenny calls you 'short stuff.'"
> "That's okay," I told him, "because Jenny is my friend."

Humor must be used with caution and good judgment. It is wrong to automatically assume that your workers personally consider you their friend. Likewise, don't make a joke unless you are certain the other person knows you are joking. Otherwise, grave and unforeseen consequences may result.

We were having an extraordinarily easy day at work. Purely in jest, I told my partner, "Oh Roseanna, you're making me work too hard!"

Roseanna refused to speak to me for several days and I couldn't understand why. At last, she cooled down enough to tell me that she felt she was carrying her share of the workload.

Do: Ask for and follow up on advice

Remember this: **Common sense is uncommon.** Your ability to find answers when none are readily available will help determine your success as a coach. Often, your best bet for answers or advice is to ask for your workers' input. When asking for an opinion, be sure to tell the other person, "Don't tell me what you think I want to hear. Tell me the truth."

As much as we workers are elated when asked for advice, we abhor seeing our input ignored. We react by thinking, "What the heck did she ask *me* for?" Then the next time we are asked, we may respond bleakly with something like, "I don't know—just do whatever you want." If you ask for advice and then don't use it, please get back to us and let us know why. Enlighten us. Then next time you ask, our advice might be of more value.

Do: Clarify information

"I know you believe you understand what you think I said, but I am not sure you realize that what you heard is not what I meant."

—*Alan Greenspan*

Messages between people can easily be misinterpreted, so make sure you get the message right when giving *or* receiving information. After relaying information or instructions, ask the other person to "feed it back to you." This way, you can be sure the other person has understood what you intended. This simple step can avoid many costly mistakes and hard feelings.

As he hurried out the bar, the manager turned to me and said, "Don't forget to chuck the oysters."

This was an order I was happy to comply with since I've always despised seafood, especially its smell, so it was with much glee that I tossed about ten trays of those stinking little sea monsters into the garbage.

After slinging cocktails all day during my tryout, the manager returned at the end of my shift to cash me out. As he did, he asked how the "Oyster Happy Hour" went. Puzzled, I told him I had done what he had asked and chucked all the oysters out. Aghast, he stepped over to the garbage can and poked around. "You chucked the oysters!" he cried. "I said *shuck* the oysters. That means to take them out of their shells. I've been advertising for weeks about our new Oyster Happy Hour!"

Instructions must be complete and accurate in order to be properly carried out. Artist Randy Glasbergen explains:

The art director told me, "We need a man standing next to a tree." So I drew a guy with blond hair standing next to a maple tree. Then I read the text after it was published and it went something like this: "His dark hair blew in the breeze as he leaned against the wide oak tree . . . "

Don't: Jump to conclusions

One thing that distinguishes seasoned, successful coaches and managers from novices is their refusal to jump to conclusions. Often, the truth in a situation lies hidden behind what appears to be obvious at first.

> On my last day at work before vacation, my roommate stopped by the restaurant to give me her share of the rent money. Because my purse was locked inside my car, I placed the cash in the register and retrieved it later on my way out.
>
> My cousins and I went to the Grand Canyon and visited my uncle Vinny in Phoenix. We had a great time, a truly memorable vacation.
>
> After I got back, I called the restaurant to find out what my schedule would be. Shelly told me that my name wasn't on the schedule. "I think you're fired," she said. "The supervisor saw you taking money out of the till."

Obtain as much information as is practical before forming a conclusion and pay no attention to rumors. Sometimes, there may not be enough information available about a situation to decide the truth. Then, you must give the benefit of the doubt. This is especially important when the situation has negative or disruptive overtones, or when the information you have is secondhand. Always ask yourself if there is a credible explanation that casts the situation in a positive light.

Do: Verify your assumptions

I do marketing analysis for an international manufacturing firm. Recently, I took leave for three weeks to undergo surgery. I was anxious to get back on the job because I wanted to establish a new Hong Kong account. Upon returning to work I discovered, to my chagrin, that a younger analyst had gotten the account. Not only was I disappointed, I was irate. I asked my team leader, "What's the idea giving the Hong Kong account to McKenzy? You should have given me the first option." The team leader replied, apologetically, "Oh, I assumed you would want to take it easy after your surgery. Hong Kong is lots of work."

I was furious. *"Assumed?"* I asked incredulously. "You mean you just **assumed**?"

She stood up and peered around the room as if looking for an answer, and then asked, "Why didn't you let me know you wanted the account? I would have given it to you."

"Well," I answered, "I assumed you would have known that I wanted it."

Assumptions are often wrong; and since they are unspoken, they too long go uncorrected. Shed a light on them by expressing your thoughts and asking for feedback.

Don't: Be judgmental

Nobody's perfect—we all have faults, even the best among us. Often, the flaws that irritate us most in others are the ones we are most guilty of ourselves. For example, impatient people are often particularly irritated by other people's impatience. Conversely, we are sometimes quick to forgive flaws that we do not share. So, next time you find yourself irritated by someone, judge yourself—not the other person.

A belligerent, uptight coach will provoke workers to behave likewise. Similarly, a strongly motivated, confident coach will inspire the same positive attitude in workers.

> My supervisor is really cool, but sometimes has a weakness of letting her fuse get short. One day after blowing up at a fellow worker, I asked her why she is so impatient with employees on occasion. She told me, "You know, anyone who really had it together, like had all their marbles in the same bag, wouldn't be working at this place."
>
> Her expression clearly told me that she realized she had stopped her mouth up with her foot. I didn't take offense though, personally, because she probably was right. While she fumbled for something to say, however, I reminded her that *she* worked here, too.
>
> "That's different," she replied, "because I'm on salary."

In life, many circumstances and opportunities are hard to control or predict. Given a slight variation of circumstances, the person working below you may have been your superior. Resist the temptation to judge people based on their position in life or at work.

We all have different priorities in our lives. To some, climbing the corporate ladder is most important. Others believe that going fishing on weekends or playing bridge on Wednesday night is what really matters. To many a job is, well, just a job. Although not everybody is equally ambitious at work, everybody wants to feel good about themselves. This is a key principle to employee motivation: help your workers to feel good about themselves.

Remind workers that they need not suffer from low self-esteem simply because they have certain shortcomings. A worker may be aware of his or her deficiencies in certain areas and yet effectively battle them simply by trying harder. With a little encouragement, this worker may even outperform those who are more skilled.

A person's self esteem and attitude can vary from day to day, according to failures or successes at work or at home. Resist the temptation to judge a person based on their behavior on any given day. Likewise, do not disregard evidence that may contradict or alter an impression you may have already formed of someone.

Keep in mind that even a judge doesn't "judge" anybody. He or she renders objective decisions based on proven facts and sworn testimony.

Don't: Condescend

A subtle, usually unspoken truth of the coach/worker relationship is that in some ways, it imitates a parent/child relationship. Like children, we want to please our coach. We want to do a good job and be praised and recognized for our efforts. The recognition motivates us to continue doing good work.

Employees sometimes act like children. For example, if "Margie" is offered a special assignment, "Jody" might become jealous. Then when Jody receives a special favor, the rest of us might each say, "What about *me?*" Though we may act childish at times, our self-esteem suffers when we are treated like children, and our motivation and job performance decreases accordingly. Listen to yourself as you speak: are you talking down to us?

> The shift manager at the restaurant where I work always treated us like children. Like, she would remind us to do things that we were already getting set to do. She would give us praise or scold us for petty little things. Some of us were nearly at the breaking point. One day when she scolded Tom for dropping a tray, he responded by acting like a kid. He made a big, emotional pout, put his head down and stomped out of the dining room. A waitress saw it happen and took the cue. She trotted over to the shift manager and said, "Shame on you! You hurt Tommy's feelings, you big, bad bully!" She was excellent, mimicking the manager's voice and mannerisms perfectly. The shift manager's jaw dropped open as the assault continued. "You go say you're sorry right now, or you will get no dessert tonight. Go on. You go apologize right this minute!"

The shift manager's face twisted in agony. She probably couldn't decide whether to fire the assertive waitress or comply with her demands. Finally, she said calmly, "I'm sorry. I didn't realize I acted like that."

After that day, things have been better at the restaurant. We are all grown up now.

Don't: Berate workers

Little external motivation is needed when workers care about what they are doing. However, it's hard for workers to care about their jobs when their supervisors are constantly putting them on the defensive. Berating workers harms self-esteem, increases stress and promotes apathy.

> Around midnight when I was about to go home from my nursing home job, the incoming supervisor called me into the dispensary. In her hand was a small envelope with *"Mr. Smith—10:00 p.m."* scribbled on it and a tablet inside.
>
> "Why didn't you give this to Mr. Smith?" the supervisor asked.
>
> "Mr. Smith was sound asleep at ten o'clock," I explained.
>
> "Then wake him up, you idiot!" she snapped.
>
> "But . . ."
>
> "Don't interrupt me!" She then delivered a long-winded tirade about responsibility, ethics, and the laws of gravity (how "stuff" flows downhill). "Now go wake up Mr. Smith and give him his medication," she ordered.
>
> "But it's a sleeping pill," I said.
>
> "Oh?" She lowered her brows and frowned. "Then why didn't you say so?"

Many "leaders" berate employees behind their backs, rather than to their faces. We are aware, when a person disparages others, that they likely do it to us as well.

Don't: Dwell on mistakes

We all make mistakes; no one needs to be reminded when they make one. Workers feel bad enough after goofing up, and generally want to prove to themselves that they can do better. Reminding a worker of a mistake or poor performance breeds resentment and deteriorates the worker's commitment to his or her job. As a consequence, the worker may be unwilling to ever go beyond the call of his or her regular routine again.

> I was a half-hour late for work one morning. That day we were short of people and the supervisor was particularly concerned about making a quota. At the end of my shift I offered to stay over for half an hour and help with the next shift. My intention, in addition to making up the lost time, was to help him make quota for the day. His blunt reply was, "You were late, and you know it!"

Mistakes should be opportunities for growth, not occasions for recrimination. Rather than dwell on a mistake, give errant workers the tools and encouragement necessary to avoid making the same mistake in the future. For more severe infractions, nothing builds trust, dedication and loyalty better than awarding a second chance.

> One day about thirty years ago I stayed late at the print shop and secretly made some joke whiskey bottle labels for my stepfather. The labels looked quite authentic—until reading the fine print!
> Next day Sid, the supervisor, found evidence of my crime, but gave me a second chance. After completing my apprenticeship, he told me that I was the best "printer's devil" he had ever worked with. I had many supervisors over the years; Sidney V. Gahan was the best of them.

Don't: Hold grudges

One morning I was forty seconds late to my workstation, even though I had clocked in on time. Clocks vary a minute or two throughout the building. I asked the supervisor to forgive me and explained that every year my family looks forward to the gift certificate the company awards for perfect attendance. She didn't listen to me and said that I should arrive five minutes early so as not to be late. Good advice, although it didn't help the immediate problem. It may have been a foolish thing to do, but I filed a grievance with the union and won. After that, she would not speak to me unless it was necessary. When she did talk to me, she had a sarcastic tone to her voice. I am no longer in her department, but sometimes I pass her in the hall and say, "Hello." She totally ignores me. It has been almost two years since the incident.

Situations like the one above are more common than you think. Even if you feel you are justified in holding a grudge, keep in mind that time should heal all wounds. People grow, develop and change. Life goes on.

Do: Give the benefit of the doubt

I am the morning supervisor at a security guard service. It is imperative that our employees reach their posts on time because we are under contract, and another guard is usually being relieved. We maintain a strict "three strikes, you're out" policy. I have heard just about every kind of excuse and do not tolerate any bull.

A recent hire was late to her post for the third time. I called her into my office after her shift and explained to her that she was being placed on suspension, which usually leads to termination. She was hesitant to offer an excuse, but when I pried one out of her she replied nervously, "I had to stop on the way and rescue two children and a cat from a burning apartment." Her facial expressions and mannerisms told me that she was lying. I did not tell her, but I decided right then to submit a recommendation for termination.

On that day's evening news, the feature story was about a "mystery lady" who rescued two infants from a burning upstairs apartment. I did not think of Sheri until they mentioned the exact time of the rescue and other details, including a general description of the lady. I called the station and *The Metropolitan News* and told them about Sheri. The City Manager recognized her with a plaque and *The News* hailed her as a heroine. Luckily for the firm, she hadn't been terminated yet. My God, that would have given us some awful publicity! What I learned from this is that people deserve the benefit of the doubt. I misread her body language. Rather than being deceitful, she was merely trying to be humble. You must take a person's words at face value—with a grain of salt at times—nevertheless, at face value. Unless there is compelling evidence that shows someone is being untruthful, you must give them the benefit of the doubt.

Do: Give recognition

"If my secretary didn't come in in the morning, I might as well go home."

—*E. & J. Gallo Winery executive Robert Gallo in* The Modesto Bee, *Secretaries' Day, 1997.*

We interviewed Mr. Gallo's secretary, and she had this to say:

Getting praise and recognition for my efforts has definitely contributed to the fact that I've enjoyed being Mr. Gallo's secretary for more than twenty years. The recognition is beneficial to my attitude and outlook. I like my job, I like working with the community, and I enjoy being a buffer between the public and Mr. Gallo's office.

Positive words of encouragement and complimentary praise work wonders for building trust and self-esteem. Many supervisors and managers, however, use superficial praise as a "Band-Aid" to patch over deficiencies in their ongoing relationships with workers. Any benefit from such halfhearted praise is short-lived. If we are treated cordially, shown respect and gratitude when appropriate, we don't need additional praise. We just need honest and deserved acknowledgment of our efforts and accomplishments. In a team setting, it is advisable to avoid awarding praise to individuals, because other workers who have worked just as hard may justifiably feel slighted.

We had complained to management that it would be nice to hear some positive words occasionally; all we ever seemed to hear was the negative. One of the middle managers took this to heart, and one day singled out one of the teletype girls for some praising. "That Peggy is one fine teletype girl. I wish we had a dozen like her. She should be an inspiration to everyone else."

Peggy was embarrassed by the remarks and the other teletype girls who all worked very hard were upset that they had been made to look inferior by comparison.

If your team has been working on a project and by good effort has completed the task on, or ahead of schedule, some kind words for the team are in order. Comment accurately on what the team accomplished, giving emphasis to the methods used to achieve its goal.

We worked super hard all week, putting in extra hours for an upcoming public tour. We were exhausted. As we were getting ready to clock out, our production manager came in and congratulated the whole team for the great job we had done by all pulling together. I felt invigorated and ready to work some more. Getting recognition, even if it's only once in a while, makes working every day more enjoyable.

There is, of course, a time and a place for "public" recognition of individual effort. Be specific and tactful, to avoid the appearance of praising one person at anyone else's expense. Highlight *what* was accomplished, and also the *way* in which it was done—pointing not only to methods but also to special skills, knowledge, and the individual intangibles of spirit, personality and character. Importantly, allow opportunities for team members to recognize one another as well, to express their mutual gratitude and support.

Recognition also is especially valuable in the aftermath of defeat. Should your workers fail to reach a goal or meet a deadline, show appreciation for their efforts nonetheless.

After losing our homecoming football game to our cross-town rivals, I thought the coach was going to line us all up and shoot us. Instead, he leaped up in the air, pumped his arm and shouted, "By golly, we played one heckuva darn good game!"

Do: Keep your promises

Too often, supervisors make empty promises. "Okay, okay, yes, yes. Now go back to work," they say, appeasing workers in the short term but not seriously considering what they have just said. Broken promises can result in irreversible damage to worker morale and dedication. The best way to make sure you keep your promises is to try not to make too many. Take notes on those that you do make so you don't forget to make good on them.

Where I used to work, each employee had to negotiate with the supervisor one-on-one for a raise. One day I met with him, explained how well I was doing, and told him that I felt I had fallen behind what I should be earning. He agreed wholeheartedly. "I wish I had half a dozen more just like you!" he exclaimed. "You'll be getting a one-dollar raise, but I can't give it to you all at once. I'll give you twenty-five cents in three months and then twenty-five cents more every three months until it's a dollar. Then we'll take it again from there."

Great. After three months and a couple of weeks had passed, I went into his office again and asked about my raise. "If I give you a raise," he said, "then I'll have to give *everyone* a raise!" What could I say? I reminded him of his promise and he replied, "You just got a raise last year. We're not doing as well this year. Nope, there's nothing in your file about any raise."

Shortly after that, I found better employment. When I told my old supervisor I was leaving, he said he really wanted me to stay and that he would get the boss' approval to match whatever pay and benefits the other place had to offer. Shaking my head, I wondered just what kind of fool he thought I was. I met his pleading gaze with this unspoken reply: "One of the benefits of working for them is that I won't have to work for *you* anymore."

Don't lie to or make empty promises to employees just to placate them in the short term. Forcing us to take a bitter pill is far better than handing us a sugarcoated placebo. We will be more likely to pull with you for the long haul if you just play it straight. If you make a promise, keep it.

Do: Follow through

A common complaint among today's workers is that supervisors and coaches sometimes fail to follow through on matters that workers bring to their attention. Employees, however, don't easily forget issues that are important enough to them to mention to their supervisors, nor do they forget when their efforts are ignored. When this happens, workers sense that their concerns are being perceived as trivial. This leads to considerable frustration, and makes workers less inclined to bring potentially highly relevant matters to anyone's attention in the future.

> Every day I have to fill out forms to account for jobs completed. I need a pencil sharpener screwed to my desk so that it won't get "borrowed." One day I asked my coach if he could get a sharpener installed on my desk. "You got it," he said. A couple of weeks later I reminded him and he said, "Oh, I forgot all about it. Sorry, it's at the top of my priorities."
>
> Now, that was about a year and a half ago. During that time my coach helped oversee the installation of a $36 million production line. Management thinks he is the greatest. But what about me? I still don't have a pencil sharpener on my desk.

The best way to keep things from slipping your mind is to take notes. Keep a list of employee concerns in a notebook, and cross them off when they are resolved.

> We used to have team meetings all the time. We would come up with some great ideas and leave the meetings all charged up. Then, poof! Nothing happens. Now we don't have many meetings and everything is still the same as it was before.

Coaches and team leaders need to delegate responsibility responsibly. Assign individuals or task teams to follow up on team proposals and ideas. Coach them to be patient—sometimes things take a while to happen. Keep the agenda open and the team well-informed on each item's status until it is completed.

Remember this: **Ideas don't work—*people* do.**

Do: Say what you mean
and
mean what you say

No one can be expected to be completely honest all the time. If you happen to feel lousy one day, and someone asks you how you're doing, you can be forgiven for saying, "Fine, thanks." It is also sometimes acceptable and understandable to lie in order to protect people's feelings. Except in these kinds of circumstances, however, you should always be forthright with workers. Realize that workers are not stupid. They can detect lies and insincerity. If you underestimate your workers' intelligence in this respect, *you* will end up looking stupid. Dishonesty dampens individual and team morale, and will end up crippling your own position as a leader—and *that's* no lie.

Our team has a split crew. Half of us normally have Fridays and Saturdays off. The other crew has Sundays and Mondays off. For upcoming holidays, we get together as a team and work out our schedules so that everyone can enjoy a three-day weekend. Our new coach arranged a weird Fourth of July schedule under which nobody got three days off in a row. In response to our many complaints, he told us that his boss had dictated the schedule to him. However, we subsequently saw posted on our bulletin board a copy of a memo *from* our coach to his boss. It read: "Mark, here is what I have decided will be the holiday schedule for the Z-line assembly team ... "

We believe that untruthfulness is one of the two most serious problems with supervisors (the other is failure to follow through). Supervisors often use lies as a weapon of convenience—to strengthen their position in an argument, to pass the buck, to placate workers' concerns, or even just to deliberately mislead.

> "There will be no overtime this Friday. Mr. Cramer told me that absolutely under no circumstances will there be any more overtime." That's what our coach told us at our team meeting after several people had asked to work overtime. I spoke with Mr. Cramer the next day. He said that he had approved overtime anytime, according to the coach's discretion. It turns out that our coach had a "hot date" that Friday. He could have just said that he had a commitment and saved himself from being revealed as a liar.

Sometimes dishonesty can cause even more serious problems. Hourly employees are at a disadvantage to salaried employees because when push comes to shove and a worker's word is pitted against a supervisor's, the salaried worker usually is given more credibility. For this reason, unscrupulous supervisors may feel they can lie to subordinates with impunity. Supervisors may also hold the arrogant belief that workers are not deserving of honest, respectful treatment. Naturally, workers can sense this attitude and may reciprocate with an equal lack of regard for the supervisor. We believe this to be the most important of all the *dos and don'ts* presented in this book. **Saying what you mean and meaning what you say is an essential element to gaining and maintaining trust.**

Remember this: **A leader does not *mis*lead.**

Don't: Manipulate

As coach, you wield considerable power over your workers' actions. Your relationship with your workers will be much more productive if you are careful not to abuse this power. Manipulation is a vulgar form of control that tears us down by creating distrust and disharmony. Rather than manipulating, try to be a positive role model to your workers. We need to be lifted up, not torn down.

Our team leader transferred to another area, and the team chose me to take her place. I believed in the company's campaign to develop teamwork and empowerment, and thought our team could make progress. The team gave me their support. Our coach was new to the job and possibly a bit insecure. I believe he considered my leadership a threat to his control. He criticized nearly everything I did and sometimes bent the truth to undermine my leadership. Our egos or personalities or something clashed, although I was only trying to do my best. I had been the team leader for about a month when a teammate reminded me of a problem that we frequently had with running out of certain supplies. She suggested that I bring it up for discussion at our next team meeting. So, I went to talk with the supplies and acquisitions coordinator to get some information upon which the team could build a discussion. He said, "Oh, I can fix that! How about if I just double the inventory levels at which the computer automatically reorders those items?" He made the changes right then.

A couple of days later the coach took me aside and told me that I really screwed up. He said that his boss (the superintendent) was extremely upset that I had gone to the supplies coordinator without going through her first. She had decided—according to my coach—that the only way to remedy the situation was for me to resign as team leader! It didn't make sense, and under considerable stress I went to talk with the superintendent the following day. After listening patiently to my explanation and apology, she said, "Oh, you didn't do anything wrong. Heck, that's exactly what I would have done. You did good—you got a problem taken care of."

I resigned anyway.

Manipulative supervisors seem to make up their own rules as they go along. They are inconsistent with their treatment of different workers when given similar circumstances.

Remember this:
Leaders don't manipulate; they cultivate.

Do: Be accessible

You need to be accessible when your workers need you, and there's no way of knowing when that might be.

> My coach is never too busy or preoccupied to give me a few moments of his time. I know that sometimes there are more important things going on, but I just can't work well when something is on my mind or bothering me. Mike always gives his full attention and tries to accommodate every need. Lots of times, he stops whatever he's doing and goes out of his way to help me out.

Sometimes an individual just needs someone to talk to. Oftentimes, you can alleviate a worker's stress and anxiety simply by being there, having an open ear and an open heart.

> I couldn't concentrate on my project anymore, so I went to talk to my supervisor about what was bothering me. I poured it all out to her, and she seemed to understand. What made me feel really good though, was how she related to a totally unrelated circumstance: she's a diabetic, just like me!

Part II

Building Teamwork

"In the interest of Teamwork and Empowerment,
I will be delegating all of my responsibilities
to the team. From now on it will be
YOUR responsibility to make
coffee and kiss up
to the boss."

Do: Delegate accountability

A group of workers without accountability is like a team of horses. Although they may be heading in the right direction, they rely on constant control and correction in order to stay on course. If left on their own, they will eventually tire and come to a halt.

Delegating accountability is one of the most difficult aspects of work team management. The word "accountability" itself has punitive overtones that incite fear in some workers. Workers do not want to be "held accountable" if a project does not work out according to management's wishes.

At the same time, workers cannot expect to achieve the status of self-direction if they are unwilling to accept responsibility, plus or minus, for their endeavors. Accountability must be given to a team in gradual, incremental steps. It must be given as concrete, positive support—not as a device for placing blame or designating a scapegoat.

Delegating accountability to a team does not mean relinquishing accountability on the coach's or management's part. Let your workers know that, as coach, you are in a direct partnership with them. Through better or worse, you are pulling with them and carrying an equal share of the burden.

In the early stages of a team's development, the coach will actually carry a lion's share of the accountability burden. Be assured, you will absorb the brunt of upper management's wrath when things go wrong.

As your team matures, accepting more responsibility will be a natural development. Workers will *expect* to be held accountable. With confidence in their work and trust in their superiors, your team members will accept a degree of accountability equal to the sum of their abilities.

Do: Set an example

My supervisor always walks around with his hands in his pockets. Whenever he comes by, the other workers make sure they look busy, then after he walks away, they just idle around and shoot the bull.

Whatever your leadership methods, you are a role model. You can't have one set of standards for yourself and another for everybody else. Set an example by always maintaining a spirited and effectual outlook.

Do: Show commitment

Although you may sometimes disagree with them, never stray from the company's goals and policies. That's not to say you should be a "yes" person—whenever you can, contribute your own input. However, keep in mind that while workers are primarily concerned with their own and their families' interests, these interests are usually best served by the company's success. "Rocking the boat" too much can set a bad example for workers; if they follow such an example, they will probably only end up hurting themselves.

Do: Build confidence

When I started here about eight years ago I tried, but had difficulty getting along with others. At the end of my probationary period, the coach showed me the results of my evaluation. He awarded the highest score for my "ability to get along with others."

At first I figured the coach was somewhat ignorant, but now I see that he has an intuitive understanding of human nature that goes beyond the ordinary.

The best way to build confidence in your workers is to believe in them yourself. Help your workers to ask not, "can we do it?" but rather "how can it be done?"

Don't: Take credit

Credit should always be given to whomever it is due. Give the team credit for team accomplishments, and correct anyone who tries to suggest otherwise. If you feel that you *deserve* accolades for your team's achievements, you are *de-serving* your team.

> Except for mistakes, my boss habitually takes credit for everything. One morning I said to him, "Nice day, isn't it?"
> He looked up at the mildly clouded sky and replied, "Yes. I'm proud to say, yes."

College Football's winningest coach, Eddie Robinson, whose teams won 408 games for Grambling University, said after his final home game, " . . . I never won a game at Grambling. The guys behind me have done that."

Do: Treat all equally and fairly

Playing favorites, holding prejudices or double standards, or not treating team members equally for any reason severely harms the development of the work team.

A lady from another department was being transferred to ours. I overheard my coach telling someone, "I don't want Karen on my team." The cards were stacked against her before she even got here. That's not fair, because anybody should at least be given a chance.

Do: Be flexible

There's more than one way to skin a cat. In the workplace, there are about as many ways to perform a given task as there are employees.

Mark was training me to operate a circuit board printer. "You stand here and take the plate like this . . . next you place it in the frame . . . and then put it in the rack . . . okay, now you try it." When I tried it and screwed up, Mark went berserk. "No, darn it! Do it like I said. This way! You do it like *this!*" I tried it again a different way and did pretty well. "No!" Mark hollered. "You're doing it backwards! Can't you pay attention? Try it again." I tried again—no problem. But Mark had a problem. He said, "Look, wise guy. I'm showing you how to do this, and I've been doing it a long time. So just do it like I showed you, okay?" I tried it the way he showed me and screwed up again. Mark stomped off and returned with Bill, the lead person.

"What's the problem here?" asked Bill.

"I don't know," I said. "I think I can do it." I gave it another try, and did perfectly.

"See," snorted Mark, "he's doing it backwards! It ain't the way I showed him!"

Bill looked at me and asked, "Are you left-handed?"

"Yeah," I answered. Then Bill told me to continue operating the machine backwards. I am now the fastest circuit board printer in the plant, even faster than Mark!

A coach must be flexible about individual attitudes as well as the team's overall vein. Award the team its requests whenever possible. If you strongly disagree with a request, don't reject it outright. If you mull it over for a while, you might find yourself becoming more flexible.

> Our team requested an extra fifteen minutes for lunch on Fridays. The coach said no way. We requested it again, and again. Every time, the coach said no way. Finally, one day he said we could try it once, but if production fell, that would be the end of it. You probably guessed it: production increased and now we have forty-five minutes for lunch *every* day!

A coach or supervisor who is used to doing things a certain way doesn't like to change. In today's workplace, however, change is vital and unstoppable. It has been decades since Bob Dylan wrote, *"The times they are a-changin',"* but those words are truer now than they've ever been, especially in the workplace. Don't block the door to change. Step aside for new and better ways of doing things.

Assure your team's flexibility as well. To remain profitable, a company must be sensitive and responsive to shifting customer needs. With an ability to rapidly shift focus and adopt new strategies, your team will help give the company a competitive edge.

To keep your workers on their toes, keep them abreast of current industry trends and future developments in the company's strategic plans. Stay up-to-date on training and maintenance schedules and be sure all supplies are available. Verify that channels of communication between teams and other departments are open, direct, and uninhibited.

Don't: Chastise the team

Share responsibility with your team when things go wrong and get down on yourself when improvements are in order. When errors occur, keep the team's accountability in perspective and avoid criticizing or placing blame. Chastising the team will weaken their will to do better, not strengthen it.

We often have coffee and donuts at our monthly team meetings. At one meeting, we decided to have a dessert potluck, and our coach gave his permission. I was biting into a fluffy slice of lemon meringue when the department manager came in and politely scolded us. "Coffee and donuts may be acceptable, but this is not. You are not to be having a potluck during your meeting times." I felt like a stupid little kid. We didn't accomplish much at the meeting, and I believe the morale of the team may have suffered.

I had a chance to talk with the department manager a few days later and told her that I thought she could have handled the situation differently. I felt she should have talked to our team leader or coach instead of ruining the meeting for everyone. She disagreed, stating that if she had something to say to anyone, she would say it to everyone involved. That made me think she felt we were all part of a conspiracy or something. Fortunately, she eventually saw things differently. She addressed our next meeting and, by apologizing, reinforced our trust in her and in ourselves.

Do: Listen and Learn

Learn to listen to your team members. If you don't listen, you won't be able to ask the right questions of them. If you don't ask the right questions, you won't hear anything *worth* listening to in response.

> Gary and Sal came over to help me in the kitchen. They said the supervisor sent them, and they asked me what to do. I told them they could scrape the freezer door, but that they should check back with the supervisor first to see if she had anything in particular that she wanted done. They began scraping the door.
>
> A while later the supervisor came by and asked why the guys were scraping the door when she wanted the walls sanitized.
>
> I explained to her that I asked them to check with her first to find out what she wanted done, but that the freezer doors needed attention. Mold was building up on the edges and anyway, I had already sanitized the walls myself.
>
> Later that year I saw the following negative entry by the supervisor on my performance review: "The chef ordered two busboys to scrape the freezer door when I had specifically sent them into the kitchen to sanitize the walls."

If you're a good listener, you'll find that you've got just as much to learn from us as we do from you.

Do: Consult and inform

Consult with all concerned parties before making a decision or setting up a plan of action. If you obtain feedback from all involved, your decision will be built upon a broad base of knowledge and a firm foundation of trust. Never skip over anyone and spring a "surprise" on them.

At our team meeting, everyone chose the project they wanted to work on. I was second in seniority and chose the "C" project because I wanted to continue working first shift. The next day a memo appeared on our bulletin board stating that all workers on the "C" project would be transferred to another office on second shift. The memo was from the district manager and dated a week earlier. I was mad, and asked the coach if I could transfer over to the "A" project, with which I had better expertise anyway. He told me it was too late, that everyone had made their choices.

"Why," I asked, "didn't you let us know about the transfer on the 'C' project ahead of time?"

He replied, "I didn't know about it until just now."

I said, "But the memo is dated a week ago."

"I know," he said. "But that was a whole week ago, and anything can happen in a week."

Then I went to talk to my department manager about this nonsense. She said, "Well, you should be grateful you could choose your own project, because Jacob can just assign you if he wants to."

Why am I telling you all this? Maybe it will get published and these clowns will read it and see themselves for the idiots that they are.

These "clowns" are not idiots, yet they can sometimes act like idiots when dealing with hourly workers. Sociologist Peter Berger offers a clue about why: "To live in society means to exist under the domination of society's logic. Very often (people) act by this logic without knowing it." The workplace, like the military or a school system, is a microcosm of society, and has its own logic. People who have internalized one system of logic find it very difficult to adjust to a new one. In the "old school" logic of the workplace, hourly workers were considered "subordinate" and were expected to do management's bidding without question. Nowadays, the old logic in the workplace is being replaced by such concepts as worker empowerment and teamwork. Bosses, however, often still instinctively act according to the old logic. They think they can engage in the kind of *doublespeak* illustrated in the above story with impunity, while indignant workers perceive it as a tactic to confuse an issue and dodge responsibility.

Try to adjust your thinking to the new reality in the workplace. Channels of communication should be free and open, honest and direct, from topmost management all the way down to the newest hourly worker. Let your workers and your superiors know what's going on in as timely a manner as is reasonable. Ask for their feedback. Give equal and objective consideration to everyone's suggestions.

Do: Endorse workers' ideas

Often, management spends little time considering team proposals that are forwarded to them. Management either gives the proposal an off-the-cuff acceptance or rejection, or shelves it indefinitely. The coach must be familiar enough with the team's needs and concerns to be able to effectively "sell" ideas to management.

> The light bulbs in our raw materials hold are always burning out and are a real hassle to replace. I suggested at a team meeting that we attach signs to the hold asking that the lights be turned off when not needed, which is most of the time. The team agreed, and assigned me to follow up on the issue.
>
> A week later, I asked my coach if he had brought the issue to management's attention. He said no, he hadn't, and agreed to let me send a memo to the department manager.
>
> "All you're doing is making people angry," the coach told me the following day. "I had already talked to the department manager, and so had Angela (the shift manager). And now he gets a memo! If you're going to declare war on an issue, make it a safety issue. Or something that concerns the team. *Light bulbs?*"
>
> That was the last I heard about that issue.

Prepare thoroughly and do your homework before presenting a proposal to your superiors. As successful salespeople know, a win-win situation must be presented. You and your team will win with a proposed idea that makes work easier and more enjoyable for your workers. But how does the company win with an idea that will cost money? When negotiating with management, you must speak the language of "dollars and sense." Show your superiors how a proposal will either make money or else save money for the company.

Recurrently, a relatively small monetary investment will pay back in intangible, hidden ways. For example, a significant improvement in working conditions may result in huge dividends for the company because of reductions in absenteeism, employee turnover and retraining costs. Sick pay and even workmen's compensation claims may be reduced. Workers who feel better about their jobs will perform better and take greater pride in their work. Better performance translates into reduced waste, greater productivity, and more profits for the company. When workers have more pride in their work, they also will produce with higher quality, resulting in increased customer satisfaction and more profits for the company.

Individual ideas and suggestions should be actively solicited by coaches and management and carried out whenever possible. All ideas should be considered; even unorthodox recommendations may have some inherent merit.

> Our company pays cash rewards for new ideas. Management always brags about the high implementation rate and about how they take every suggestion seriously. I'm not too good at coming up with ideas, but submitted a suggestion (seriously) that a monkey could do my job.
> About four months later, my coach walked me out to the receiving dock and showed me a god awful monstrosity from GMF Robotics. "There's your monkey!" he said. Then he handed me an envelope with twenty-five bucks in it.
> I'm still trying to think of another suggestion.

Don't: Impose quotas

It is natural for individuals and work teams to have good and bad days. If you try to regulate productivity by imposing arbitrary quotas, you take away the flexibility and freedom that would allow workers to think creatively and experiment with innovative methods. Workers who must adhere to quotas tend to stick to familiar methods and generally maintain the "status quo," since meeting the quota is all that's ever expected of them. As a result, team empowerment and continuous improvement are inhibited.

Workers are resentful of quotas, which rob them of individuality and give them little reason to care about their work. Under quotas, workers are taught to care more about quantity than quality. With little pride in what they do, workers may end up pushing any old thing down the line.

Of course, management must assure the company's productivity, and won't tolerate the absence of production goals of any kind. The coach should negotiate with management on his team's behalf to establish flexible, independent production goals. Workers get more pleasure out of surpassing their own goals than management's, and are therefore likely to be more productive if they are allowed to participate in the establishment of their production goals. Work teams should be made privy to sales forecasts and other managerial information, so they can be as well informed as possible about how to set realistic and meaningful goals. If a coach—or management —determines that a quota system must absolutely be maintained, there may be a deeper problem with motivation and leadership that should be studied and remedied.

I worked at a sawmill in Missouri several years ago. Our site foreman was a quota nut, insisting on eight trucks of lumber being processed each day. "Eight loads a day keeps the boss away," he often said. We usually made the quota, unless, as frequently happened, fewer than eight trucks arrived, in which case we would either stretch the work out or go home early. Sometimes the foreman had to turn trucks away when too many arrived; they would head for another mill or make an appointment for the following day.

One Friday morning a freezing rain fell throughout our part of the Ozarks. When the logging trucks arrived at the mill, the logs were frozen together, and separating them was nearly impossible. By noon we were really far behind, with only our third truck about halfway unloaded. The site foreman ordered us to work through lunch because we had to be finished before five o'clock. He then drove off to the boss' house for lunch, as he always did.

Now, the whole situation had me fuming. I was nearly crying in pain from the icy weather and physical demands of prying those logs loose and loading them onto the chain. I hopped on a forklift and unloaded all of the trucks, just dumping the timber on the cold, muddy ground. Then I went home. I would surely get fired, but I had had enough.

Nobody works at the mill on Saturdays, so I was darned surprised to see the site foreman at my doorstep the next morning; I was even more surprised when he asked me to come to work.

His face was red with embarrassment. "When I got back from lunch yesterday, everyone was gone!" he said. "Someone dumped all the timber over the sides. Come on, we've got to go pick it up and run it."

Truthfully, I couldn't afford to lose my job. The whole crew was there when I arrived, and we did what needed to be done. Afterward, the site foreman treated us to a case of beer and we had an informal meeting where we all aired our gripes and devised a plan to deal with them.

The "quota system" ended. A monthly bonus took its place, by which we could receive extra pay for exceeding the old quota average. During the remaining eighteen months that I worked there, I received a bonus check every month. We often unloaded twelve trucks in a day, and almost never had fewer than eight trucks arrive. We developed a reputation among the loggers as a mill that would unload their trucks quickly, and we became their mill of choice for the area.

I consider it quite ironic, yet logical, that when the site foreman finally turned his attention and loyalties toward his workers, production increased dramatically.

Rather than doggedly following fixed quotas, establish a "continuous improvement task team," empowered to recommend better, more efficient ways of doing things. The task team may question whether a certain step or procedure is really necessary. The team may engage in studies of topics such as costs analysis, supplies availability and the effects of absenteeism. They may also look for ways to improve product quality and customer satisfaction. Any relevant information should be made available to the team on request. Allow the task team a role in carrying out any of its recommendations that receive management's approval.

Even though management is usually involved in some kind of efficiency study of its own, it's a good idea for a task team to investigate this area as well. A redundancy of efforts is not detrimental to continuous improvement; on the contrary, it helps management make well-balanced, well-informed decisions.

Do: Seek the consensus

How exactly should empowered work teams make decisions? The easy way out is to take a team vote. This approach has major shortcomings, however. First, the issue on the table may not have been studied or discussed thoroughly enough. Secondly, those who vote for the minority position may feel alienated, and seeds of dissent may sprout.

It is better to seek a consensus than to take a vote. Explore an issue as completely as possible. Look for alternative solutions and encourage everyone's participation. Individuals will then begin to understand and adapt to each other's views, and everyone will gain a broader perspective on the issue. Occasionally, the consensus decision may in fact be to let a vote decide the question. The important thing is to include everyone in the process as much as possible.

> We were totally taken in by the charisma of our team leader. She provided initial direction, then had her own ideas about what the team should be doing. We have gradually become disillusioned, while she now aims primarily to enhance her own image in the eyes of management.

Work teams will often, predictably, elect their most charismatic and popular member to the role of team leader. Subsequently, the team may simply go along with all of the leader's ideas and suggestions, allowing him or her to make all the decisions. When this happens, the team will eventually lose direction and stagnate. This predicament is best avoided by laying out in the team's initial ground rules that the leadership will be rotated periodically. As coach and mentor, work one-on-one with your team leader to "spread the wealth" of leadership and always seek the team consensus.

Don't: Place blame

Who did it? It usually doesn't matter. Finding solutions is what matters.

> One day we were just about ready to clock out for the weekend when the shift supervisor came running in, yelling, "No one clock out! No one clock out, we're having a meeting." She was running around like crazy, making sure everyone heard her. At the meeting, she dropped a stack of spreadsheets on the table with an obvious mistake on the top one. "Who did this?" she asked. "Everyone's in deep trouble until I find out who did it."
>
> I grabbed the top sheet and took a close look—it was mine! Everyone gawked at me. "I did it," I confessed.
>
> The supervisor glared at me and said, "It figures it would be a temp worker!" She told me that my work was unacceptable and to not bother coming back to work Monday.
>
> Upon returning the page to the stack, I noticed that the next page had the same mistake. I thumbed through and discovered that *every* page had the same mistake! Something must have been wrong with the net server that day, but I kept mum.
>
> At first I wasn't planning to, but I came back to work on Monday, and now I am a permanent employee!

Although there is usually no need to place blame, no one will blame you if you take responsibility yourself.

> Between tracks on the Mamas and Papas' compact disk, *Sixteen Greatest Hits*, singer Cass Elliot comes in late to a group harmony. As the

music falls apart, John Philips, the group's leader and coach, says, "You're late coming in."

Mama Cass replies, "I was right with you."

"Sorry, my mistake," Philips says. With no further delay, the group then goes on to record the "take" version of *Midnight Voyage*, which subsequently became a substantial hit for the group.

True leaders have the strength, maturity, and self-assurance to not only admit when they are wrong but to swallow their pride and take responsibility when things go wrong, regardless of the "facts."

Always avoid forcing others into a defensive posture; resentment will result, along with a diminished degree of care about what they are doing. Phrase questions and comments in a positive, supportive manner rather than in a critical or confrontational way. Instead of asking a subordinate, "Why is this report not finished yet?" ask, "How's the report coming along?"

Sometimes the source of a recurring problem or conflict can be pinpointed to a single individual. In order to resolve the problem, the individual must be shown that a problem exists, without being blamed for it. The individual must then be persuaded to internalize his or her role in the problem and be given the opportunity to participate in its solution.

Your team, likewise, must learn to internalize any "team" problems. Recognizing that there is a problem and defining it accurately are the first steps to solving any problem. Placing blame will only hinder the problem-solving process.

Do: Nurture individuals

"If you really want to be a successful leader, you must develop
other leaders around you. You must establish a team."

—*John C. Maxwell*

Widen your workers' skills and leadership abilities, and they
will reward you with a more confident and productive work
team. You can learn a lot about individuals' aptitudes and
potential through casual conversation. You may discover that
an individual has a talent for computer programming or a
strong mechanical aptitude. Workers often have potential in
areas that they are not even aware of.

As you become familiar with your team members and gain
confidence in their abilities, exploit their untapped potential
and latent skills by giving them new challenges. They will
gain invaluable self-confidence and job satisfaction from rising
to the demands of their new tasks. However, keep in mind
that challenging team members with work that they do not
possess the necessary skills for can have the opposite effect.

Conversely, some workers may have weaknesses in certain
job areas. Find ways to give them practice in those skills
without assigning "busy work" or setting them up to fail. Be
patient and bring them along at a manageable pace.

Inevitably, you will encounter an employee who lags behind
in team/cooperative spirit. What separates you, as leader,
from that employee is your ability to bring about change in
others. You must have the patience to remain fair and

impartial. Talk straight with that person and avoid using any manipulative strategies. You can't hammer attitude changes into anyone; attempting to do so will only cause that person to further withdraw. What you *can* do is reinforce any positive behaviors through regular contact and active, supportive coaching. Without placing blame or accusations, accurately define and objectively discuss any particular problems that need to be addressed, inviting the worker to participate in finding solutions. Limit your efforts to one specific problem at a time. Behavioral changes may be in order and will usually bring about changes in attitude—a person who *acts* more professionally will take on a more professional outlook. Instead of viewing the problem employee as a weak link in the chain, consider the maxim, "what makes one look good makes everyone look good." As other team members progress and strengthen their partnership, lagging individuals will develop a natural desire to catch up and come into the fold.

Provide continuous on-the-job training and periodic retraining to keep your team members' skills current. Encourage and arrange cross-training within your department, as well as with other departments in the company. Workers will better appreciate their own jobs and be more cooperative with others when they understand more fully how their work fits into the overall picture.

Additionally, encourage outside schooling and education. Many companies will pay the costs of community college classes or night school in areas such as computer literacy, oral communications, and English as a second language, in order to improve an employee's skills at work.

Do: Delegate sparingly

You should delegate enough work to your team so that your time and abilities are most efficiently spent. However, do not delegate simply in order to place extra burdens on others and lighten your own load. A coach, like the captain of a ship, should be able and willing to perform any of the work he assigns. Delegate thoughtfully, by considering which tasks give workers needed breaks from the monotony of their usual routine and which workers are able and willing to take on additional responsibility. Also, don't "pick on" the same people to always do the same jobs; spread the work around as evenly as possible.

My office supervisor gave me the task of delegating the weekly summary to my teammates. Each week, I picked someone new to do the job. I thought it was an honor to do the weekly summary, and that everyone would be anxious to have their turn. When I asked Edward to do the summary, he said, "What are you picking on me for? I didn't do anything."

At our next team meeting, I asked if anyone wanted to volunteer to do the weekly summaries. Everyone raised their hands except Edward. He looked around shyly, put his head down, and then raised his hand.

Don't: Push your own agenda

One day we got a new supervisor for the processing department at the poultry plant where I work. He was hired from outside the plant, but knew the business very well. He was energetic but perhaps overzealous. In a short time he initiated many new programs and innovations. His pet project, however, didn't mesh well with the company mindset, which has always been to maintain the highest standards of product quality.

His goal was to increase the weight of every chicken by 2 percent. We tried steaming them before putting them into the ice water bath; we tried steaming them afterward, and in stages in between. In essence, he was trying to sell processing water for the price of chicken meat (I have seen this trick work at construction supply yards, where they soaked sand and gravel with water in order to increase the selling weight). Chickens proved to be quite resistant to soaking up water, although we did achieve some success.

When upper management discovered our supervisor's scheme, they fired him instantly.

A coach's job is stressful enough as it is. Don't compound your stress by trying to force-feed your own program to your team. Be sensitive to what the team needs and wants to do. Keep in mind what is best for the company, and go with the flow.

Don't: Micromanage

"Never tell people how to do things. Tell them what (needs to be done) and they will surprise you with their ingenuity."
—*George Patton*

Work teams require neither a charismatic wonder person nor Attila the Hun to provide motivation. When given a clearly defined task with a sense of importance, well-trained workers will organize themselves effectively when left to their own devices. Supervisors often stifle workers by trying to manage every aspect of their jobs.

> I was busy sweeping the floor, pushing all the debris into a huge pile. My supervisor came by and pointed at the pile and asked, "Are you going to pick that up?"
>
> "No," I said, "I'm just gonna leave it there." It took Mr. Goofus several seconds to realize that I was only joking. Of course I'm gonna pick it up!

Some coaches believe that they are good delegators simply because they know how to tell others what to do. In fact, they are more like *dictators* than delegators. Delegating responsibly often means *not* telling us what to do. When we are dictated to, we become resentful and perform tasks grudgingly. When given the authority to plan, perform and perfect our own work, we take greater pleasure in our work, and often discover additional things that need to be done and better ways to do them.

"What are you doing?" I asked. A layer of filth, dust bunnies and food scraps littered the floor.

"I'm mopping the floor," Martha said.

"Well, shouldn't you sweep it first?" I asked.

"No, the supervisor just told me to mop the floor," she answered. "And anyway, since when did they make *you* a supervisor?"

Exchanges like the sarcastic confrontation above occur frequently in workplaces where each employee is under direct supervisory control. Such control breeds bad attitudes and low self-esteem. Cooperation is strained, because workers become accustomed to serving one master rather than helping one another. In a less-controlling, team-oriented environment, the encounter would have gone something like this:

"Let me help you," I said. "I'll get a broom and sweep, and you can mop behind me."

"Oh, thanks," Martha smiled.

As coach, your job is to clearly define with your workers what needs to be accomplished and to negotiate outputs with them. The team must feel that the task is important enough to be worthy of its enthusiasm. Give your workers authority to plan, perform and perfect their own work, according to ideas and methods they are themselves familiar with or able to obtain knowledge about. Help them to cut through any barriers and offer assistance should they encounter difficulty. Then, stay out of the kitchen while the cooks do their thing.

Remember this:

The art of coaching involves being in control without controlling.

Do: Discourage competition

Some old-fashioned supervisors believe they can increase production by encouraging workers to compete against each other. This may be true in certain cases and in the short term. In the long haul, however, competition within a company, by inhibiting cooperation and innovation, is detrimental to continuous improvement. Workers will hoard technical information and keep helpful tips to themselves. If a competitive rating system exists in your department, get rid of it.

> Charlie said that he got to be supervisor by always being in "competition" with other workers. By always outperforming everyone else, he rose above them. He suggested that I follow the same philosophy. I tried it for a while, and soon found out that the other workers weren't playing the same game. They just let me do more and more of the work.
>
> Since then, I have discovered that the best way to increase my own productivity is by helping those around me to increase theirs also.

Many organizations give recognition to individual workers with programs like "Employee of the Month." These programs run counter to team development. Replace them with a system that emphasizes cooperative team methods that are in place and being used to improve product quality, efficiency and customer satisfaction.

Remember this:
Cooperation always beats the "competition."

Do: Be persistent

Being tough *is* tough; it's not easy to be assertive and persistent without seeming pushy. To accomplish any task or mission, or to effect change within your department, you may have to keep pushing for a long time. This area is another reason why successful coaching is a delicate skill. Keep focused on your vision and expect results, but don't *demand* them. Perseverance must be balanced with patience in order to bear fruit.

Remember this: **Patience carries a lot of *wait.***

Do: Prevent conflict

An ounce of prevention is worth a ton of cure. Preventing conflict between workers is vastly preferable to resolving conflict after it occurs. Conflict inflicts wounds that leave long-lasting scars.

Conflicts are especially common when workers are tense and under stress. The best way to prevent conflict is to reduce stress in the working environment. The following are a few suggestions for reducing stress and conflict among workers:

- Keep individual and team goals reasonable and attainable.

- Be sure that workers' duties and responsibilities are clearly defined, that they understand why particular procedures are in place, and that all necessary tools are available.

- Encourage team members to openly share their knowledge with one another and to exchange ideas, techniques and helpful tips. Coach individuals to avoid being offended when another worker offers a suggestion, points out an error, or has an alternate opinion.

- Discuss methods of conflict resolution at team meetings, and conduct periodic classes or discussions on the subject.

- Try to maintain a positive relationship between your workers and upper management. Workers who feel good about their bosses usually get along better with each other. Arrange for your superiors to attend team meetings occasionally to acknowledge the team's contributions to the company's success and to host open-forum discussions.

- *Never* express any criticism of anyone in management, other coaches, or members of your work team. An atmosphere of personal criticism around your team will not only add to workers' stress, but will undermine your ability to lead, and ultimately increase your own stress level.

- Study principles of interactive communication, leadership, and Total Quality Management from a variety of sources.

- Downplay conflicts that do occur. When your work team is operating smoothly, in a cooperative spirit, conflicts will be very rare but are sure to arise occasionally. When they do, don't be too alarmed. If at all possible, allow workers to resolve their differences on their own, one-on-one—this builds and reinforces trust. Usually, the biggest challenge is getting the conflicting parties to meet.

- Assign people who get along well with each other to work closely together. Workers are usually more productive, more creative, and maintain a more positive attitude when working alongside those with whom they get along well. In larger work teams, there will inevitably be times when two or more workers do not get along well with each other. Just as oil and water do not mix, certain individuals may be naturally incompatible when working in close proximity. While it is not always possible to keep incompatible workers apart, don't force the issue by deliberately throwing them together and expecting them to overcome their differences. That approach is counter-productive, and only invites conflict.

A tense situation can flare into conflict when a person who feels he or she has been wronged receives sympathy and support. Most people instinctively offer sympathy to people who are upset. In doing so, they may be unwittingly adding fuel to a fire. When a person gets a shoulder to cry on, their emotions tend to become stronger, because the sympathy they receive has the effect of affirming and validating their position. This sympathetic reinforcement can blow a volatile situation out of proportion.

Rather than giving sympathy and support, it is better to downplay and rationalize a tense situation. If "Mary" approaches you and complains, "Sean keeps bumping into me on the line," don't build up Mary's anger by saying, "Yeah, he bumps into me all the time, too!" Instead of sympathizing, downplay and rationalize. *Empathize* with Mary and say, "That must make you feel uneasy. He's probably not doing it on purpose though. I'll have a talk with Sean and ask him to watch out for you. In the meantime, you can help out by watching out for him as well."

An important idea to understand is that future conflicts can be prevented by effectively resolving present conflicts as they occur. When a conflict arises, first give your workers the opportunity to resolve their differences by themselves. The coach should only arbitrate (not intervene) if necessary. If you consider it necessary to arbitrate a conflict, allow sufficient time for cooling off. Those involved will then see things more clearly and, in all likelihood, will be more eager to resolve their differences.

Try this method and adjust it to fit your style . . .

Arbitration Method of Conflict Resolution

❶ Meet at a neutral location, neither your office nor either party's workstation.

❷ Place blame for the conflict on circumstances, not on the people involved. For example, perhaps their schedules have been tough, causing tension and stress, or maybe they were obligated to work on a weekend when they would rather have been at home. Look at the situation and try to find out what circumstances may have contributed to the conflict or caused it in the first place.

❸ Explain that both parties are responsible to some degree for allowing a conflict to develop and that they must share equally the responsibility of resolving the dispute.

❹ Ask one person involved to describe the nature of the conflict and to suggest a solution.

❺ Ask the other person (or the person representing the other side in the conflict) to describe the nature of the conflict and also suggest a solution. Ideally, the conflict will be resolved after step four or five. If not, go on to step six.

❻ Ask both sides to allow you, the coach, to arbitrate the conflict with a decision that both sides will honor. (If both sides do not concur, you should find someone else to mediate whom everyone agrees upon.)

❼ Ask any questions (who, what, why, when, where, how) that may be necessary for you to obtain enough information to see the situation as clearly as possible. Formulate your questions so that they require explanations, rather than simple "yes" or "no" responses.

❽ Your decision may involve an oral evaluation of the conflict, or it may require a course of action. Take as much time as necessary before rendering your decision. Feel free to dismiss the meeting and decide on the matter later. Once the conflict is in your hands, it will be largely defused. Rather than each side remaining angry with the other, at worst one side or both will reroute their anger—to some lesser degree—toward you. You can handle that, and soon any bad feelings should fade because everyone will realize that you were fair and did the best you could.

Conflict resolution is most difficult when the conflict involves untruthfulness on one side or the other. Unless you have irrefutable reason to believe which side is telling the truth, you must give *both* the benefit of the doubt. In most conflicts, the truth resides somewhere in between the opposing views. When mediating such misunderstandings, try to find ways in which both sides are right *or* both sides are wrong. Seek common ground that at least partly justifies everyone's position.

If you cannot find any common ground in the dispute, you must grind out a compromise that both parties will agree to. Though this is inherently disadvantageous to the truthful party, both sides should respect you for being fair. Compromising initiates a healing process that will be completed when the parties ultimately learn to forgive and forget.

One day at work a woman got mad at me because of something I said to someone else. She made up a bunch of false charges against me and turned me in to management for harassment. She claimed to have two witnesses to back her claim that I shot her in the face with my air gun. Utter nonsense. I confronted her about that and she held firmly to her story. So, I was forced to defend myself against her claims before the division manager.

After hearing my denial, the division manager said that the woman in question may have exaggerated her stories, but asked me if it were possible that I may have accidentally shot some air in her direction without being aware of it. "No," I replied. Nothing of the sort had ever happened.

The conflict went unresolved for more than three years, during which the woman and I avoided each other entirely. Then, at a class about conflict resolution, we were taught that in most conflicts, both parties must share a portion of the responsibility.

I believed that she was entirely responsible for the conflict, not me. She was the one who perpetuated the false charges. Then I realized that the woman had reminded me, almost subconsciously, of someone else I knew long ago who had done me wrong. As a result, I had been unfriendly to her without being aware of it. Her harassment claim was only a reaction to the way I had been treating her all along. So, in a way it was my fault.

I explained to the woman that she reminded me of someone else and that I had treated her unfairly, as if she were that other person. "It was my fault," I said, "that we had problems in the past, and I would like to apologize."

"Well, it was my fault too," she said.

Our conflict is finally over and we get along quite well now.

Sometimes a controversy may have its roots in an unrelated circumstance from the past, or complex psychological factors may be at play. It's impossible to completely resolve every conflict; some can only be defused and given over to time for healing. It is vital, however, that all disputes be sufficiently rectified so they do not interfere with the functionality of the work team.

> I was driving to K-Mart one evening when this guy in a Blazer began tailgating me. After a while, I pulled over so he could pass. The guy pulled up next to me and stuck his head out the passenger's window and hollered, "Pull over next time, beech! Let a guy pass, you dumb slow-poke." I was scared he was going to get out and hit me or shoot me or something. Thank goodness he drove off. I knew I'd never forget that guy's face.
>
> About a week later, I was transferred to my company's downtown division. They introduced me to my new associate, and it was the guy! He didn't recognize me, but he probably noticed my nervousness. When I told him about the incident, he denied it, saying it must have been someone else.
>
> Other people in the office say that Chuck is the nicest guy. He really is good to people at work, and maybe he was just having an extraordinarily bad day when we first crossed paths. I don't like to carry a grudge, but I just don't feel comfortable working with Chuck. What should I do?

Pitting one person's word against another's has the potential to escalate a conflict and make resolution impossible. There is usually little or no need to decide who is telling the truth. Two people may view an event from entirely different angles, with each believing their view to be correct. What is important is that the incident be put to rest, not for anyone to necessarily be the winner or the loser.

Your course of action in such disputes may be to simply bring the two people together and have them shake hands. This symbolic gesture works. Even though the parties may only grudgingly participate, if they agree to let go of the past and start anew, a healing process will have already begun.

Do: Assess Progress

A work team develops through many stages (forming, storming, performing, etc.); for general discussion, a team's progress can be defined within three broad categories.

Dysfunctional: A dysfunctional work team is one that has regressed, failing to keep up with a company's historical production standards. Workers are inhibited by a lack of focus and leadership. Employees will tend to say "they" when referring to company goals and projects ("When are *they* going to add the new export division?"). The most common cause of a team becoming dysfunctional is being ushered into the empowerment process at too fast of a pace. A team in this predicament needs a facilitator or facilitation team to work with it. A full-time coach may be necessary to guide the team to the next level.

Functional: A functional work team is one that continues or betters a company's historical production standards. Goals are set by the team and most decisions are arrived at by consensus. The coach's role is to patiently assist the team in its development toward the next level, which may take several years.

Self-directing: A self-directing work team is one that has learned the nuts and bolts of project development and implementation. Leadership is spread throughout the team, communications channels are uninhibited, and continuous improvement is a driving force. Employees will say "we" when referring to company goals and projects ("When are *we* going to add the new export division?").

When workers achieve self-direction, it does not mean that management will abandon them and leave them entirely on their own. To the contrary, managers will forge an even stronger relationship, a true partnership, with their work teams. As coach, you will be in a position to guide your team up toward the *next* level, which is as unlimited as your own vision and imagination.

To assess the progress of work teams, some companies issue an annual questionnaire. They tally up the answers and, if there has been an increase in positive responses over the previous year, they conclude that their work teams have made progress. The value of this process on the team level is questionable. Teams must self-evaluate their progress as well.

Progress assessments should be done periodically. Ask the team leader to manage an assessment in the manner of a brainstorming session. Team members should identify and acknowledge all areas that they have made improvements in, be it in production, helping others, or anything at all. Discuss ways to improve on the improvements. Likewise, bring any shortcomings, hindrances, or other problems to light. Entertain all suggestions about how to make things better. Obtain a consensus at each session on a plan of attack to make progress in a limited number of specific areas.

Epilogue

Carl Sagan once said, "The person making a claim is responsible for proving it." Some claims and principles expressed in this book are supported by the testimony of the accompanying stories and anecdotes. Some are reinforced by a logical basis, often no more than a single sentence in length. Many *dos and don'ts* in this publication merit an entire chapter to themselves, with supporting statistics and other types of proof. However, we feel that approach would have resulted in laborious reading. We believe most of the fundamentals presented in this book—to borrow a phrase from a somewhat more famous document—to be self-evident. The principles are therefore presented briefly, for your consideration and contemplation.

Nevertheless, nothing in this book is carved in stone. Work team dynamics is a relatively new field and we welcome any comments and suggestions, or alternative viewpoints. Ultimately you—the reader, our customer—are the boss. Please E-mail or write the publisher with any comments, suggestions, or workplace-related stories.

Now, you deserve a break. We have collected a few insightful stories from the workplace for your enjoyment . . .

Part III

Mini Stories

"And then, that reminds me
of the time when . . ."

The Little Cactus that Could

by Kelly McClymer

I work for an office that continually adapts its policies to changing attitudes. We try to see that individuals with disabilities don't get left behind and can keep up with "regular" workers. Our emphasis has always been to focus on what supports individuals need to achieve their goals, and to provide those supports.

On my birthday last year, the staff bought me a pretty, purple cactus. I like cactus plants because you can sort of neglect them, water them occasionally, and they do all right. After a few weeks though, this plant started to smell terribly.

Some staff thought there was a dead mouse somewhere. I didn't want to throw the plant away because it was a gift, but when everyone finally knew that the little cactus was stinking the place up I threw it in the trash. "Wait a minute," my supervisor said. "Let me take it home with me. I'll repot it and give it some TLC." I felt a bit guilty because maybe the poor cactus would stink up her house. Mostly, though, I was relieved to be rid of the rotten thing.

Three months later she brought it back in. She had nourished it well, and a big, beautiful flower had grown from the tiny cactus! All it needed was love and attention and a little extra water. Over the years, I have seen many employees transformed from pitiful cacti into fully developed flowers by the skills of our wonderful supervisor. No one better or more clearly illustrates the credos of our workplace—labels can stunt growth, and with the right support anyone can blossom.

The Unorganized Manager

by Tag Goulet

As a part-time management communications instructor at the University of Calgary, I like to show my students films which illustrate important management fundamentals. Many of the films make their points by showing what *not* to do. Normally I book my films months in advance. But one semester, after starting a hectic new management job, I found myself leaving my university duties until the last minute.

One day, feeling even more overwhelmed than usual, I called to book a film for the next evening's class. The university administrative assistant answered in her usually efficient manner and I began, "Hi Doris, it's Tag. Sorry for the short notice. The film I'd like to show tomorrow is—" I stopped, suddenly realizing the title of the film was lost in a pile of paperwork on my desk.

"Hang on Doris, it's in here somewhere," I said, shuffling through papers as she waited patiently on the line. "Aha!" I finally exclaimed, finding the title after what seemed like an eternity of digging through documents. "The film I'd like to show this week is, *The Unorganized Manager.*"

Internal Housekeeping

by Jen Ryan

I was having trouble with one of our trainees, who despite my efforts to discourage the habit, was inclined to simply bury any work she felt incapable of dealing with.

This "out of sight, out of mind" mentality had resulted in important documents being hidden at the bottom of her "In" tray, dispatched to random corners of the store cupboard, and even sent anonymously around the region by internal mail.

After several unsuccessful attempts at guiding her into better work practices, I realized I was going to have to address the issue directly.

My opportunity came one morning as I was sweeping the hallway inside our building. An assault of flu had left us desperately understaffed, and for the day, I was filling the most junior position in the firm, as well as my regular job.

"Oh, Annie," I said, as our trainee approached with a form requiring my signature. "I've been wanting to talk to you." Uncomfortable with the task ahead, I quickly read and signed the form, then returned to my sweeping.

"It seems you've been having trouble coping with some of the more challenging aspects of your work," I began, pushing my pile of dirt toward the doorway. "I've tried to explain to you, Annie, just how important it is to deal with all your work as it comes along." I worked the dirt to the edge of the doorsill and swept it back into a manageable pile again.

"This inclination to simply hide things, rather than going through the correct procedures, even asking for help if necessary, has got to stop." I opened the door and held it with my foot.

"Do you understand what I'm saying, Annie?" I asked, drawing the broom back for one last stroke. "It's very important to do the right thing, and I think in your heart you know that." Turning to face Annie, I said, "Have I made myself clear?"

"So, what you're saying," Annie said slowly, gazing through the doorway, "is that you should do the job properly, not just sweep your problems out the door."

"Absolutely," I replied.

"Ms. Erickson?"

"Yes, Annie?"

"Would you like me to show you where we keep the dustpan?"

Confidence Game

by Donna Bush

I was the assistant store manager for a specialty retail establishment. Our particular location did the highest volume of about seventy stores in the chain. It was high pressure sales, all day, every day. My boss was very demanding and critical. She must have been hired for her marketing and organizational abilities, not her people skills, which were virtually nonexistent. My job was to handle all personnel issues, including looking after the morale of the staff.

Last Christmas was the toughest ever. She and I were the only salaried managers left in our store because the others had either quit or gone to other locations. I felt that the only way we were going to get through the season would be to have a heart-to-heart talk about the way she makes me feel when she talks down to me. After all, it's difficult to promote morale among your staff when the boss makes you feel like an idiot.

I told myself I wasn't going to cry and tried calmly to explain to her what I didn't like. I was diplomatic, almost apologetic. I emphasized that I realized we had different views on things, but that it shouldn't prevent us from working together to keep the store running.

Everything went fairly well until I got to the part where I told her I didn't like her talking down to me. Tears welled up in my eyes and I couldn't help but let a few fall. My voice was low, but steady, and I looked her in the eye. "I just want you to know how you make me feel. You talk at me like I'm a third grader and I resent that you don't treat me with professional respect."

As I tried to quickly compose myself, I thought at last she would understand how difficult and painful it was to work with her. I was being straight with her, exposing myself and my anxiety, while giving her a perfect opportunity to be supportive at last.

Her response? "You know what your problem is? You take things too seriously. You wouldn't feel this way if you didn't put this kind of pressure on yourself. I didn't want to say anything before because I didn't want to contribute to that pressure you already place on yourself. You seem unable to find any confidence in your abilities."

I was floored. After I opened myself up to her in an effort to ease the tension of being shorthanded in the busiest season of the year, she tells me it's all in my head. She just blows me right off, exposes my vulnerability and tells me it's my own fault. Great. What a confidence builder! I stuck it out through Christmas. However, once the new year came and there were suddenly two new managers in the office, I couldn't get out of there fast enough. When I told her I was resigning to pursue my writing career, she laid it on thick and told me how happy she was for me.

When I told the staff individually that I was leaving, each of them was supportive and offered encouragement. One person asked if it was difficult to walk away from something I had been doing for nine years. I thought about that Yuletide conversation with my boss.

"No," I replied, "it's not as difficult as I thought it would be."

"Wow," she said, "I wish *I* had that kind of confidence and courage."

Any Openings?

by Jennie L. Phipps

I was once in charge of hiring personnel for a medium-size, family-owned company. One of the owners was an unobtrusive little man with a desk in a corner office removed from where the rest of us worked. He was a grumpy soul with little to say except on those occasions when something pushed his buttons and he sent off a nasty missive. I had been on the receiving end of a few and they made me do whatever I could to avoid having anything to do with him. We were having some remodeling done on the building and as you must know if you have ever remodeled, the jobs can take forever. In fact, a few of the workers had been around for so long I began to get friendly with them. One of them was an amiable sort whom the construction supervisor seemed to use as a "go-fer." One day I got a memo from the owner describing this fellow and complaining that the job was taking too long and it was probably this fellow's fault, since he didn't seem to know much about the construction business. Coincidentally, on the same day, the fellow wandered into my office and asked if he could put in an application. I said, "Sure. What do you want to apply for?" He said he wanted a job just like the guy in the little office. He said he had been watching that guy for six weeks and had never seen him do anything. It was, he said, a job that he was sure he could handle!